CLASSIC BIBLE STORIES
THE OLD TESTAMENT

retold by Lise Caldwell
with art from the Standard Publishing Bible art collection

D1742317

STANDARD
PUBLISHING
Cincinnati, Ohio

ADAM AND EVE

Genesis 1–3

God created a beautiful world with oceans and sky, plants and animals, and a man and a woman. He called the man Adam. Then he took a rib from the man's side and made a woman. He called her "Eve." He placed Adam and Eve in a garden called Eden, and said, "You may live in this garden and enjoy its beauty and its fruit. But you may not eat from the tree in the middle of the garden."

The serpent said to Eve, "Why don't you eat the fruit from the tree in the middle of the garden? It looks delicious."

"God said that if we ate from that tree, we would die," Eve replied.

"No," lied the serpent, "You will not die. God just doesn't want you to be smart like he is." Eve saw how good the fruit looked, so she took some and ate it. Adam was with her, and she shared some with him. Then they realized they were naked, so they hid. Adam and Eve had to leave the beautiful garden, because they disobeyed God.

NOAH AND THE FLOOD

Genesis 6–9

People began to forget about God and to do wicked things. Only one man, Noah, pleased God. The Lord told Noah that he was going to cover the whole world with a flood. He told Noah to build an ark and bring his family and all different kind of animals on board.

Noah built the ark just as God had told him to do. God brought the animals to Noah, then Noah, his family, and the animals got on the ark. It rained for forty days and forty nights. At last the waters began to go down. Noah sent out a dove to see if the bird could find anywhere to land. That evening the dove returned with an olive leaf in its beak! God told Noah and his family to come out of the ark.

God promised never again to flood the whole earth. He made a rainbow and told Noah and his family to remember that promise every time they saw a rainbow in the sky.

ABRAHAM AND SARAH

Genesis 12, 15, 17, 18

Once there was a man named Abraham who had great faith in the Lord. The Lord told Abraham and his wife Sarah to go to a special country called Canaan. The Lord was going to give the country to Abraham and Sarah and their children. Abraham and Sarah did as the Lord told them, but they never had any children.

One day, when Abraham was almost one hundred years old, some men came to visit him. He offered them some food and water. They sat down together, and the men told Abraham that when they came back in one year, Abraham and Sarah would have a baby. Sarah heard them and laughed. She thought she was too old to have a baby. But she and Abraham did have a son. They named him Isaac, and thanked God for their special baby.

Joseph's Dreams

Genesis 37, 39–46

Jacob had twelve sons. One of his sons, Joseph, was very special to him. Jacob gave Joseph a beautiful coat to wear, and Joseph's older brothers were jealous of him.

One day Joseph told his brothers about a strange dream. "We were binding sheaves of grain in the field," Joseph said. "Suddenly my sheaf stood up, while all of yours gathered around me and bowed to me." Joseph had another dream in which the sun, the moon, and eleven stars bowed down to him.

His brothers grew very angry when Joseph told them his dreams. They wanted to kill him, but instead they sold him as a slave to Egypt. In Egypt Joseph obeyed God and grew very powerful. When there was a famine in Canaan, his brothers came to Egypt to buy grain. Joseph gave it to them, but they did not recognize him. Then Joseph told them who he was. His brothers brought their father, Jacob, to Egypt and they all lived there together.

THE EXODUS

Exodus 1–14

Joseph's family stayed in Egypt and got very big.
Then a Pharaoh began to rule who did not like the
Israelites. He made them slaves. The Israelites
cried out to God and God sent a man named
Moses to lead the Israelites out of Egypt.

Moses and his brother Aaron went to
Pharaoh and asked him to set the Israelites free,
but Pharaoh said no. God sent ten plagues on
the Egyptians. At last Pharaoh let the Israelites
go. The Israelites gathered their belongings and
left Egypt.

But Pharaoh changed his mind. He and his
armies pursued the Israelites. The Israelites came
to the Red Sea, but had no way to get across. They
were terrified, because Pharaoh's chariots were get-
ting close. The Lord told Moses to raise up his
staff. Then the waters of the Red Sea parted, and
all the people crossed on dry ground. When
Pharaoh's armies came, the walls of water came
down on top of the soldiers, but the Israelites
crossed in safety.

THE FALL OF JERICHO

Joshua 1–6

When Moses died, Joshua became the leader of Israel. He took the people across the Jordan River and into the promised land. The first city the people saw was Jericho. Jericho was a large city with a powerful army. The Lord promised Joshua that the Israelites would conquer it. The Lord told Joshua to take all the armed men of Israel and march them around the city once a day for six days, and on the seventh day to march around the city walls seven times, with priests blowing trumpets. The Lord promised that if the Israelites did this, the walls of the city would fall down and Jericho would be theirs.

Joshua did just as the Lord said. He was strong and very courageous. On the seventh day, with a mighty shout, the walls tumbled down. God gave the city to the Israelites!

GIDEON'S 300 MEN

Judges 6, 7

Once a huge army of Midianites went to war against the Israelites. A man named Gideon was leading the Israelites. He gathered an army of thirty-two thousand men to go to battle, but the Lord said to Gideon, "You have too many men."

"If anyone is afraid to fight," Gideon said, "he may go home." Twenty-two thousand soldiers left.

Then the Lord said to Gideon, "You still have too many men." So Gideon took the men to get a drink of water. Three hundred men lapped the water with their hands to their mouths. The rest knelt down. "Take the three hundred men into battle," the Lord said.

Each man held a torch in his left hand and a trumpet in his right. They smashed the jars that covered their torches, shouting, "For the Lord, and for Gideon!" Blowing their trumpets, they ran down into the army camp. The Lord gave the Israelites the victory!

DAVID AND GOLIATH

1 Samuel 17

The Philistines had a giant warrior named Goliath. Every day he would say to the Israelites, "If anyone is brave enough to fight me, step forward. If he defeats me, we will be your subjects. If not, you will be our slaves!" No one was brave enough to accept Goliath's challenge.

When a young shepherd named David went to take food to his brothers in the army, he heard Goliath's dare. "I will fight the Philistine!" David declared. Everyone thought he was crazy. King Saul gave David a suit of armor, but the armor was too big for David. David took the armor off and went to fight the giant with only five smooth stones and a sling. Goliath made fun of David when he saw him approaching, but David said, "I will fight you in the name of the Lord God!" David took a stone, slung it, and struck Goliath in the forehead. Goliath fell on his face, and the Philistines ran away in fear. God made David a hero!

KING SOLOMON

1 Kings 1–8

David's son Solomon became king when David died. Solomon asked God for wisdom, and God made him the wisest man who had ever lived. Many of Solomon's wise words are written down in the book of Proverbs.

David had wanted to build a temple for God, but the Lord told him, "Your son will build it." The Lord kept his promise. He allowed Solomon to build a temple in Jerusalem. The temple of the Lord was beautiful. Solomon placed the ark of the covenant inside it. He dedicated the temple to the Lord in front of all the people.

"O Lord, you are the one God," Solomon declared. "We know this temple cannot contain you, for you fill the heavens and beyond. But please watch over us and listen to the prayers we make in this temple." Solomon offered sacrifices to God and worshiped him.

DANIEL IN THE DEN OF LIONS

Daniel 6

Daniel was one of the Israelites captured and taken to Babylon. King Darius put Daniel in charge of the whole country. The other servants of King Darius became jealous of Daniel. They went to the king and said, "You are so wonderful that we think you should make a law saying that no one can pray to anyone but you for a whole month."

"So be it," said the king. "Anyone who disobeys will be thrown to the lions." The men were delighted. Daniel heard the decree, but went to his window to pray to the Lord God anyway, just as he always did. The men saw him praying and ran to tell the king. The king was sad, because Daniel had to be thrown in the den of lions at sundown. When morning came, the king rushed to the den and shouted to Daniel, "Has God rescued you?"

"Yes, he has!" replied Daniel.

The king was overjoyed. "Daniel's God is great," said the king. "I decree that everyone in my kingdom must respect the Lord God."

QUEEN ESTHER

Book of Esther

Once a king named Xerxes ruled in Persia. Xerxes chose a beautiful woman named Esther to be his queen. Esther was a Jew, but her uncle Mordecai told her not to tell the king.

A high-ranking official named Haman hated Mordecai, because Mordecai would not bow down to him. Haman went to the king and said, "The Jews do not obey your decrees. Will you let me have them killed?" Xerxes gave him permission.

Haman ordered that on a certain day, all the Jews were to be killed. Mordecai heard about this and sent a message to Esther. "What can I do?" Esther asked. "The king has not asked to see me for a month, and if I go without being invited, I could be killed!" But she was brave, and she went to see the king. He was delighted to see her. She told him about Haman's plot to kill her people. The king was very angry with Haman. The Jews were saved, thanks to brave Queen Esther.

Look for these other products featuring Standard's Classic Bible art collection:

Classic Bible Stories, A Family Treasury (03848)

Classic Bible Stories, The Life of Christ (04257)

Classic Bible Stories, The Old Testament: Coloring Book (22045)

Classic Bible Stories, The Life of Christ: Coloring Book (22046)

Classic Bible Stories, A Reproducible Coloring Book (02255)

12 Classic Bible Art Teaching Pictures: Old Testament (02290)

12 Classic Bible Art Teaching Pictures: Life of Christ (02289)